JUST THE JOB!

I work as a Park-Keeper

by Clare Oliver

Photography by Chris Fairclough

W
FRANKLIN WATTS
LONDON · SYDNEY

© 2002 Franklin Watts

First published in 2002 by
Franklin Watts
96 Leonard Street
London
EC2A 4XD

Franklin Watts Australia
56 O'Riordan Street
Alexandria
NSW 2015

ISBN: 0 7496 4203 3
Dewey Decimal Classification 363.6
A CIP catalogue reference for this book is available
from the British Library

Printed in Malaysia

Editor: Kate Banham
Designer: Joelle Wheelwright
Art Direction: Jason Anscomb
Photography: Chris Fairclough
Consultant: Beverley Mathias, REACH
REACH is the National Advice Centre for Children with Reading
Difficulties. REACH can be contacted at California Country Park,
Nine Mile Ride, Finchampstead, Berkshire RG40 4HT. Check out
the website at **reach-reading@demon.co.uk** or email them at
reach@reach-reading.demon.co.uk.

Acknowledgements
The publishers would like to thank Lisa Curry and the
staff at Sir Thomas & Lady Dixon Park, Belfast, the
Parks & Amenities Department at Belfast City Council,
pupils and staff from Cabin Hill School, Knock,
and Valerie Christie, for their help in the production
of this book.

Contents

Meet Lisa   6

Beds and Borders   8

Stocking the Beds   10

Indoor Work   12

The Rose Garden   14

The Japanese Garden   16

Nature Trails   18

Through the Seasons   20

Pros ...   22

... and Cons   24

Finding a Job   26

Glossary   28

Find Out More   29

Index   30

(Note: words printed in **bold italics** are explained in the glossary.)

Meet Lisa

Do you like being out in the open air? Lisa does! She works as a park-keeper, which means she is outside all day long. She can listen to the birds and look at the beautiful trees and plants.

This is Lisa. The public park where she works covers more than 50 hectares.

Of course, Lisa doesn't have much time to relax. She has an hour off for lunch and a couple of tea breaks, but the rest of the time she has to work hard in the park. She arrives at 7.30 a.m. and stays there until 4.30 p.m. She works Monday to Friday, but at busy times of the year she might do weekend overtime.

Lisa is responsible for keeping her areas of the park looking their best for visitors, especially the rose garden. She has to mow lawns, plant borders, and prune shrubs and hedges. Lisa has to keep the weeds and bugs under control, too. It's a very demanding job, but Lisa enjoys it.

Stephen and Kenny also work at the park. Kenny is the park manager. He tells the others which jobs to do. ▼

The park puts on a rose show each July, but the rose garden needs to be tended all year round. ▼

Park-Keeper

JUST THE JOB!

Lisa's daily tasks depend on the weather and the time of year. They include:

- Clearing away dead plants
- Hoeing to get rid of weeds
- Digging *fertilisers* into the soil
- Putting in new plants
- Spraying to get rid of pests
- Pruning shrubs and clipping hedges
- Raking up leaves
- Mowing the lawn

Beds and Borders

Much of the park where Lisa works is made up of woodland and rolling lawns. The main area of **bedding plants** is in the walled garden. Lisa works hard to keep the borders here looking neat and colourful.

Favourite Five

Lisa's favourite parts of the park are

1. The rose gardens
2. The walled garden
3. The Japanese garden
4. The rhododendron walkway
5. The wildflower meadow

Gardening equipment is transported around the park on the back of a tractor.

The team in charge of parks at the city council faxes special planting plans to the park. That means that Lisa knows what to plant – and where.

Lisa digs over a bare bed before stocking it with new plants.

Lisa goes to the greenhouses to select new plants for the empty beds.

Once a display is past its best, Lisa removes the plants one by one with a fork. Then she digs over the bed, adding some fresh rotted manure to the soil at the same time. Now the soil is rich, crumbly and ready for more plants.

Hoeing helps to keep the weeds at bay.

Lisa has to look after the current displays, too. **Deadheading** means plucking off any dead flowers. Lisa also weeds the beds, by hand or with a hoe.

Stocking the Beds

New plants are cultivated in the greenhouse. Sometimes Lisa helps plant up new trays of seeds. Lisa likes being able to stock the flowerbeds in the park with plants that she has grown.

> Lisa waters the seed trays using collected rainwater, not tap water. ▶

Top Tips

Here are Lisa's tips for bringing on young plants:

1. **Don't plant seeds too deeply.**
2. **Never overwater – but don't let trays dry out, either.**
3. **Thin out the seedlings to avoid overcrowding.**
4. **Be gentle when *transplanting* seedlings.**
5. **Never allow young plants to outgrow their pots.**

First, Lisa fills the tray with special seed compost. Then, using a small stick, she makes furrows or lines called *drills*. Different seeds prefer drills of different depths, so if it's a seed Lisa has never planted before, she reads the packet carefully. She sprinkles the seeds into the drills and then gently covers them with a little more compost. Finally, she sprinkles on some water.

10

As the seedlings grow, Lisa removes plants that look weak and straggly in order to give the stronger plants more space. This is called thinning out. The remaining plants soon outgrow the tray, so Lisa transplants them into bigger and bigger pots to give their roots room to grow.

Lisa gives each new seedling a marker label, so that it can be easily identified.

Eventually, the young plants grow big and strong enough to be planted in the flowerbeds outside.

Lisa piles up some compost and uses it to fill the bigger pots as she transplants young plants.

Indoor Work

When the weather is poor, Lisa tries to find indoor jobs to do. She might spend some time in the tool store, for example. Each worker in the park has their own set of tools. Lisa makes sure hers are all free of mud, and uses an oily cloth to clean the metal parts. She also checks that her wheelbarrow runs smoothly. If it doesn't, she adjusts the wheel or fits a new one.

Essential Kit

Lisa keeps her tools in tip-top condition. She dries them off after using them in the rain, so that they don't rust. Her tools include:

- **Spade**
- **Fork**
- **Trowel**
- **Hand fork**
- **Rake**
- **Hoe**
- **Pocket knife**
- *Secateurs*
- **Hedge clippers**
- *Pruning saw*

A nother job for rainy days is helping out at the **botanical gardens** down the road. Lisa likes spending time in the Palm House, a large glasshouse open to the public. The Palm House can get quite hot and steamy. That's because it has displays of **tropical** plants, which need those conditions. Sometimes, Lisa helps with the watering in the Palm House.

This is the Palm House. It has beautiful displays of tropical plants all year round.

Lisa uses a hose to water the schizanthus plants inside the *humid* Palm House.

The Rose Garden

The park where Lisa works is famous for its roses. Since the 1960s, it has held a Rose Week each July. There are hundreds of different types of roses. The gardeners try to make them all bloom in this one week.

Lisa checks that the shrub roses are labelled properly ready for Rose Week.

As well as weeding the beds, other jobs include feeding the plants and pruning them into shape. The climbing roses clamber over **pergolas**. The park-keepers have to tie in their growing shoots to direct where they grow.

Stephen ties up the climbing roses to stop them getting tangled.

Fertiliser for the roses comes in pellets. Lisa wears gloves to sprinkle them on the ground. ▲

Some roses are prone to disease, such as black spot, rust or powdery mildew. **Aphids** can attack them too. That's why the plants are sprayed with a mixture of **fungicide** and **pesticide**. Lisa wears a special suit so that she doesn't breathe in the spray or get any on her skin.

Lisa sprays the roses to kill any fungi or insect pests. She wears protective clothing for spraying. ▲

Favourite Five

Lisa's favourite roses are:
1. 'Madame Hardy' (pure white)
2. 'Ingrid Bergman' (velvety red)
3. 'Tequila Sunrise' (yellow edged with red)
4. 'Southampton' (apricot yellow)
5. 'Blessings' (salmon pink)

The Japanese Garden

One of the attractions at the park is the beautiful Japanese garden. It has only been there a few years. Now that it has been planted, it does not need much attention. Stephen is responsible for this area, and he goes to check up on it now and again.

Stephen wears wellington boots when he is clearing weeds from the pond.

Its main feature is a large, shallow pond dotted with stepping stones and boulders. Different types of pondweed grow in the pond, and Stephen makes sure that no single type becomes overgrown. If it does, he wades in to pull it out by hand or with a stick.

Litter spoils the view. Stephen picks up any he finds.

The plants in the garden include tall bamboos and *specimen* maples. Bamboo clumps need thinning every year or two to stop them from spreading. The maples don't need looking after, but in autumn they drop plenty of leaves for Stephen to rake up.

The gravel in the Japanese garden needs to be raked to keep it smooth.

Stephen loves the maples' deep-cut, delicate leaves. In autumn, they turn vivid red or yellow.

Japanese Garden: Style Tips

- Bamboos – dramatic grasses that rustle in the breeze
- Gravel – raked into gentle swirls to look like water
- Water – to reflect the sky and surrounding trees
- Koi carp – precious fish that dart through the shallows
- Boulders – to represent mountains, but in miniature
- Moss – to make soft, shady mounds of velvety green
- Maples – trees grown for their bark and autumn colours
- Hostas – plants with handsome, heart-shaped leaves

Nature Trails

The park has a nature study centre that helps local schoolchildren to get the most out of their visits. Robert, the education officer, runs the centre. Lisa gets on well with Robert. She likes to talk to him about the park's wildlife.

Sometimes the nature centre organises wood-carving days for the public. Look at this beautiful badger!

At the start of a school visit, Robert talks to the group about the animals and plants in the park. He has a special box of tricks that contains lots of different objects for the children to touch – including dead creepy-crawlies and a stuffed hedgehog.

In warm weather, Robert takes the nature table outside.

Robert shows the children the wildlife in the study centre pond – tadpoles, pondskaters and whirligig beetles.

Next, Robert leads the party around the park on a nature trail. There are plenty of pauses for special activities. Sometimes the children do bark rubbings or collect fallen leaves for art projects. Or Robert might give them a checklist of things to look out for and tick off. No two visits are ever the same.

With Robert as their guide, the school party takes a nature walk.

Education Officer

JUST THE JOB!

There are lots of different ways to become a park education officer like Robert. One is to take a degree in a subject such as *Environmental* Studies or Geography and then a teacher-training course. Robert's tasks include:

- **Promoting the park through special events**
- **Leading nature walks**
- **Producing information pamphlets**
- **Giving talks in local schools**
- ***Conservation* work**

Through the Seasons

The jobs Lisa does change through the year. Spring is the time for re-seeding the lawn or old beds. All the summer bedding plants go in, and the lawns get their first mow. From now until the autumn, the grass needs cutting once a week.

Lisa is planning to re-seed this bare patch of lawn.

During the summer, the main job is keeping the displays looking their best. Borders and beds are weeded and sprayed. As flowers fade, Lisa deadheads them. None of the plants are watered, but a **mulch** of composted bark or manure helps to keep in the moisture.

In late spring Lisa removes the hyacinths from the walled garden when they have finished flowering.

In autumn, Lisa plants spring bulbs and puts in winter bedding plants. She rakes up fallen leaves, and gives the lawn some well-needed beauty treatment.

Top Tips

With so many visitors tramping over it, the grass needs serious looking-after. This is Lisa's autumn turf maintenance programme:

1. Lisa spikes the lawn, making holes so the soil can 'breathe'.

2. Lisa rakes the ground very hard to pull out moss and dead grass. This is called *scarifying*.

3. Lisa sprinkles on a top dressing of sand, lawn feed and moss-killer.

Autumn is mulching time. Lisa forks on a layer of rotted manure.

In winter, she digs over the *herbaceous borders* and also creates new beds. The frost helps to break up the soil. Lisa tidies the edges of all the borders with edging shears.

21

Pros ...

For Lisa, the very best part of being a park-keeper is being outside. Lisa likes being active. She would feel very restless if she had to sit at a desk all day. All the physical labour keeps her fit, too.

Lisa loves the smell of freshly-cut grass. ▼

Lisa feels lucky to work in such a beautiful environment. ▼

Lisa likes planting things and watching them grow. Every day she sees how the park's visitors appreciate the gardens. This gives her a real sense of achievement. She also likes being able to enjoy the park quietly in her spare time. There are birds, squirrels and other animals to see.

Lisa has lots of fun with the other park-keepers. Many jobs have to be done as a team, and Lisa likes being able to talk to the others while she works.

> It's nice getting to know the regulars. Lisa often stops to say 'hello' to people walking their dogs in the park.

She also likes her working hours. Starting so early wouldn't suit everyone, but Lisa knows it means getting home early too. She also gets 25 days of paid holiday, a **pension** and free training if she wants it.

Because she works for the council, her job is graded according to experience. Being told when she has gone up a grade makes it easy for Lisa to track her own progress.

... and Cons

The weather is probably the biggest drawback to Lisa's job. There's snow and ice in winter, and rain most of the year round! But Lisa likes her job least in the height of summer, when it can be almost too hot to do anything.

> Bad weather is a big downside to Lisa's job. Even a waterproof won't keep off all the rain.

Essential Kit

Lisa wears a uniform, so that visitors to the park can identify her easily.

- Sweatshirt with the park's logo
- T-shirt to go underneath
- Blue work trousers
- Yellow waterproof jacket for rainy days
- Steel-toed workboots
- Protective suit, gloves and mask for spraying
- Ear protectors for noisy work

It makes Lisa happy to see visitors enjoying the park, but sometimes she gets irritated when she sees people dropping litter. Most dog owners are responsible, but not everyone clears up after their animals – and dogs that aren't kept on a lead can wreck a flowerbed in minutes.

Another problem is that it can be dirty work. It's easy to get cuts and scratches from the roses and other plants and there are itchy insect bites to worry about in the summer. Lots of bending can leave Lisa tired and achy by the end of the day, but she doesn't mind. After a soak in a hot bath she soon recovers.

Digging over the beds is hard work, but worth it. It keeps the soil in good condition.

Lisa's job includes heavy work – like heaving this wheelbarrow off the tractor.

Of course, some of the work that Lisa does is dangerous, and she has to handle sharp tools. But Lisa has been properly trained to avoid accidents, and she always wears protective clothing for spraying.

Weedkiller is poisonous but Lisa's suit protects her.

The main **qualifications** for being a park-keeper are that, like Lisa, you enjoy being outside and working with plants. You will also need training. Lisa did her three years' training at the council training centre, but most higher education colleges run **horticulture** courses too.

An important quality is liking things to be tidy. Lisa takes great pride in her neatly-pruned yew walkway.

There are often college students on *work experience* at the park. Stephen is showing Colin how to plant the new summer bedding.

For the first three months of the course Lisa went to college every day, but after that she only went in for one week each month. The rest of the time she was gaining hands-on experience at six-month placements in different parks. Most people on council-run courses are offered a job in a public park when they finish.

Job Know-How

What qualifications do I need?

An NVQ in horticulture or similar.

What personal qualities do I need?

Happy outdoors, hard-working, knowledgeable about plants and how to care for them, responsible, fit and strong, good in a team.

How do I apply?

Approach your local council's Parks Department to find out if they run any courses, or apply to a local college. You could also ask in your local park to see if there are any odd jobs you could do without training, just to gain experience.

Will there be an interview?

Yes – to see how well you will fit in. Most parks are looked after by only a small team of people, so it's important that people work well together.

Kenny keeps a close eye on his team, and lets them know when he is pleased with their good work.

Competition to get on a course can be fierce. It's a good idea to be able to show that you are a keen gardener. Why not take photographs of work you have done in a garden or on an allotment. Find out as much as you can by reading magazines and books about gardening.

You'll also need to show that, like Lisa, you are strong enough to withstand the physical work, so make sure that you keep fit.

27

Glossary

Aphids	Bugs that feed on plant juices and carry plant diseases.
Bedding plants	Plants big enough to go in a flowerbed; usually these are annuals, which means they flower once and are then thrown away.
Botanical gardens	Places that display special collections of plants, often from hot parts of the world.
Conservation	Looking after wildlife and the environment.
Deadheading	Plucking off dead flowers.
Drill	A shallow row made in a seed tray, for planting seeds in.
Environment	Surroundings.
Fertiliser	Something (such as compost, manure or pellets) that adds goodness to the soil.
Fungicide	Chemicals that kill off fungi and fungal diseases such as black spot.
Herbaceous border	A border that contains perennial plants – plants that die back in winter – and that may include herbs.
Horticulture	The growing of flowers, fruit and vegetables.
Humid	Describes warm, wet conditions.
Mulch	A layer of material (such as straw, manure or bark chippings) that is put on top of the soil around the plants to suppress weeds and keep in moisture.
Pension	Money paid to someone when they have retired (stopped work).
Pergola	A wooden frame, used as a support for climbing plants.
Pesticide	Chemicals that kill off insect pests.
Pruning saw	A small, handheld saw, used for cutting through branches that are too large for secateurs.
Qualifications	Official requirements for a particular job.
Scarifying	Using a metal-toothed rake to scratch at the surface of a lawn and pull out moss or other unwanted materials.
Secateurs	Small pruning shears.
Specimen plant	A special variety of plant, grown for display.
Transplanting	Moving something and planting it somewhere else.
Tropical	From the part of the world closest to the Equator.
Work experience	An unpaid period of work, often for a week, so that a person can see what a job is like at first-hand.

Find Out More

Visit the park where Lisa works:

Sir Thomas & Lady Dixon Park
Upper Malone Road
Belfast

Find out more about further qualifications by visiting the NVQ website:

www.dfee.gov.uk/nvq

Visit this website to find out about all sorts of outdoor careers:

http://www.ceg.org.uk/info/Animals ,+Land+and+Environment.htm

There are lots of magazines specially for people interested in gardening. Look in your local newsagent for:

BBC Gardeners World
Garden News
Garden Answers

Read this book to find out about the history of public parks in Britain:

Public Parks by Hazel Conway (Shire Garden History)

Join this society to learn more about plants and gardens and to find out about local gardening clubs:

Royal Horticultural Society (RHS)
80 Vincent Square
London SW1P 2PE

As an RHS member, you will also receive their monthly magazine:

The Garden

In Australia and New Zealand you can check out:

NSW National Parks & Wildlife Service
www.npws.nsw.gov.au/about/ careeropp.htm
World National Parks Links
www.atn.com.au/parks/links.htm

You can also contact your local council offices or local polytechnic to find out about courses.

Also, why don't you...

• Visit your local library and check out the careers section. You could also look for books about gardening or parks.

• Find out if there is a teacher at your school who is an expert careers advisor.

• Look in your local telephone book to find out the names of parks in your area, and then contact them about work experience placements.

Index

borders 7, 8, 20, 21
botanical gardens 13, 28

children 18–19
climbing roses 14
compost 10, 11
council 8, 23, 26, 27

deadheading 9, 20, 28
digging 7, 9, 21, 25
dogs 23, 24

education officer 18–19
equipment 8, 12, 25

fertiliser 7, 9, 15, 28

greenhouse 9, 10–11

hedges 7, 26
hoeing 7, 9
holidays 23

insects 7, 15, 25, 28

Japanese garden 8, 16–17

labels 11, 14
lawns 7, 8, 20, 21, 22
litter 16, 24

manager 7, 27

nature study centre 18–19
nature trails 19

overtime 6

plants 6, 7, 8, 9, 10–11, 13, 17, 20, 21, 22, 26, 27, 28

pots 10, 11
protection 15, 24, 25
pruning 7, 14, 26

qualifications 19, 26, 27, 28, 29

raking 7, 17, 21
rhododendrons 8
rose garden 7, 8, 14–15

seasons 20–21, 24
seedlings 10, 11
seeds 10
soil 9, 25
spraying 7, 15, 20, 24, 25

teamwork 23, 27
thinning 10, 11, 17
tools 12, 25, 28
tractor 8, 25
training 23, 26, 27
transplanting 10, 11, 28
trees 6, 17
tropical plants 13, 28

uniform 24

visitors 7, 22, 23, 24

walled garden 8, 20
watering 10, 13
weather 7, 12, 24
weeds 7, 9, 14, 16, 20
wildlife 6, 17, 18, 19, 22
work experience 26, 28, 29
working hours 6, 23